Backyard Catapults
How to Build Your Own

Backyard Catapults
How to Build Your Own

by Bill Wilson

Loompanics Unlimited
Port Townsend, Washington

Neither the author nor the publisher assumes any responsibility for the use or misuse of information contained in this book. It is sold for informational purposes only. Be Warned!

Backyard Catapults
How to Build Your Own
© 2005 by Bill Wilson

Cover by Nick Bougas
Interior illos and photos by Bill Wilson

Published by:
Loompanics Unlimited
PO Box 1197
Port Townsend, WA 98368
Loompanics Unlimited is a division of Loompanics Enterprises, Inc.
Phone: 360-385-2230
Fax: 360-385-7785
E-mail: service@loompanics.com
Web site: www.loompanics.com

ISBN 1-55950-246-0
Library of Congress Card Catalog Number 2005928237

Contents

Introduction 1

Chapter One:
Catapult History...5

Chapter Two:
Build a Base 19

Chapter Three:
Build an Onager...31

Chapter Four:
Build a Trebuchet 53

Chapter Five:
Build a Ballista 57

Chapter Six:
Beyond Fun and Games...77

Final Thoughts 83

Resources...85

Introduction

Welcome to ***Backyard Catapults: How to Build Your Own.***
Nearly five years ago, I wrote a small booklet entitled *Build a
Catapult in Your Backyard*. It was so successful that popular
demand required me to revise and expand it significantly, with
new and better illustrations, new weapons, and new insights
into the nature of mechanical artillery.

This book is the culmination of a lifelong dream: to build a
weapon in the spirit of the war machines of the Greeks and
Romans. As a little boy I would watch movies about ancient
battles. I loved it when the catapults were brought out. I would
watch them toss boulders into the path of charging soldiers or
at castle walls. And I would dream about having one for my
very own.

Like so many little boys, I never quite grew up. In my mid-
thirties I saw a program on the Discovery Channel about a
group of British experimenters who built a modern version of
a trebuchet, a medieval catapult. The next day I went to
Lowe's and wandered the store for hours, looking at materials
and letting my imagination put together a weapon that could
be built for little cost, using supplies found at any home
improvement or hardware store.

Soon after that I sat down with my brother, a carpenter,
woodworker and, like myself, a perpetual adolescent. We
sketched out designs and traded ideas. Then we went
shopping. The result was the machine shown in the first

edition. In terms of firepower, it can toss a standard-sized masonry brick approximately one hundred yards. It is simple to build and fun to shoot. Is it safe? Well, I haven't gotten killed yet.

Since that book was published I've continued my experiments and developed new designs. The result is improved construction methods and several new weapons. One is a modern version of the ballista, an ancient Roman device that fired spears. The one you'll see here shoots blocks of wood. However, it can also fire bolts mounted with metal heads. It can impale a human being. This is a serious weapon that would come in handy if your home or business were ever besieged by a rioting mob.

You'll also see how to construct a trebuchet, which uses a counterweight to toss its ammunition in a high, wide arc. These were first developed in the Middle Ages to bring down castle walls. The medieval versions were monstrous in size, capable of tossing huge boulders hundreds of yards. Mine is smaller and throws hand-sized rocks about fifty yards. If you're looking to build something just for fun, and the range you can toss things is limited by property boundaries or other restrictions, this is the way to go.

I've greatly expanded the historical section as well, tracing the development of these weapons from their humble beginnings to their decline in the latter Middle Ages. In addition I've included a chapter for survivalists and others who may actually want to use these devices in real combat. In a scenario where civilization breaks down and small tribes of humans are pitted against each other, knowing how to build and use the projects in this book could spell the difference between survival and annihilation.

There's something in these pages for history buffs, weapons aficionados, and kids of all ages. So turn the page, and enter the fascinating world of mechanical artillery. Thanks for coming along on the journey. I hope you enjoy it as much as I.

Chapter One
Catapult History

There are only a couple of species on the earth that conduct organized warfare: ants and human beings. Of these two life forms *Homo sapiens* have been by far the most inventive in finding new ways to kill each other. From early battles fought with clubs and stones we've "progressed" to guided missiles and hydrogen bombs.

Early on, men realized that muscle power was of limited use in combat situations. Even the stoutest Cro-Magnon could only swing a stick or toss a spear with so much force. With the development of fortifications the balance of power swung to the defenders. Forces greedy for their neighbor's bounty needed a way to break down city or castle walls. This led to the development of the earliest forms of catapults.

(Mechanical artillery pieces have been given a variety of names throughout the ages, as we'll see throughout the book. However, for simplicity purposes, I'll be using the collective term "catapult" to refer to the different types on and off throughout this book.)

Four hundred B.C. saw the development of the first true forms of mechanical artillery. The Greeks built enormous crossbows that could fire bolts several feet long. Historians tell us that they could rip through as many as four or five of the enemy at a time! Thus the earliest catapults were used for anti-personnel rather than anti-fortification purposes.

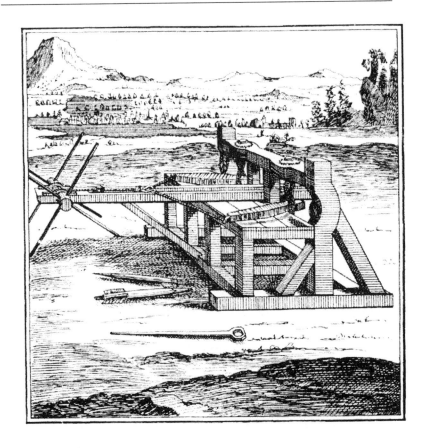

Figure 1-1

As effective as this device was, it soon became clear that it was not effective against stone walls. To meet this challenge rock throwing weapons were invented soon after. See Figure 1-2:

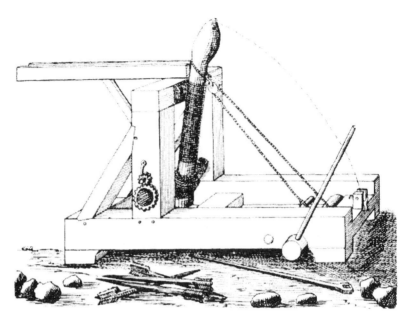

Figure 1-2

This is what most people envision when they think of a catapult. It used elastic cords made of animal sinew and hair wrapped around the throwing arm to fire heavy stones. These were launched against built up defenses such as log or stone walls. With repeated firings even the strongest defenses could be reduced to rubble.

When the Romans conquered Greece in 146 B.C. they adopted the Greek catapults for their own uses. The Empire made great use of these weapons. The Roman historian Vegetius tells us that each cohort (a division of Roman infantry consisting of approximately 300 men) was equipped with a catapult. A legion (a division of anywhere from 3,000 to 6,000 men) carried ten stone-throwing catapults and sixty portable ballistas that launched spears up to six feet long.

The stone-throwing catapults soon earned the name "onager" meaning "wild ass." The historian Procupius tells us that this was because its rear end would buck up and kick backwards upon firing, just like the aforenamed animal would do to drive away dogs and other critters that disturbed it. At first these devices held their ammunition in a giant "scoop" resembling a large wooden spoon. But the Romans soon realized that replacing it with a sling gave the weapon far more range.

Just how far could an onager shoot? It's well known that they had greater range than the archers of the day, who could fire an arrow up to 280 yards. Most historians believe the average catapult could toss a fifty pound stone anywhere from 350 to 400 yards, with some exceptional ones able to fire up to 450 yards.

Its Achilles heel was its size. Although smaller onagers could be pulled by animals, it was often necessary to build the larger ones on the spot the battle was to occur. The Romans employed combat engineers to travel with their infantry. Their job was to build catapults of sufficient size and power when the soldiers arrived at the military objective.

Because this was a time-consuming task the really large weapons were reserved for laying siege to walled towns. Such an operation was long-range in nature and afforded the attackers the time to build truly massive catapults, capable of tossing stones a hundred pounds or more an appreciable distance.

The portable ballistas proved devastating against the Celts when Rome invaded Britain. The ancient British forces were disorganized bands of locals strung together in loose coalitions. They were much like the American Indian confederations that resisted the European conquest of their continent centuries later.

Their tactics were simple and their morale easily shaken. When an iron-tipped bolt was fired at them traveling at 115 mph (by modern estimates) they would scatter in terror. Archaeologists have found skeletons of ancient Brits with ballista spears buried in them.

The stone throwing catapults were of less value in Britain, but remained a deadly part of the continental Roman forces until the Empire's collapse in 476. As barbarian forces sacked the once mighty city they not only took gold, jewels and other goods but also knowledge of Roman weapons and tactics. History tells us that the Vikings used catapults to besiege Paris in 885 A.D.

During the Crusades siege warfare was developed to a fine art. The European forces often found it necessary to assail a Muslim-held castle or fort. As they conquered territory they built their own castles to secure their hold on the captured lands.

Castles of the day were nearly invulnerable. They usually consisted of heavy stone walls several feet thick, with defense towers located along the perimeter of the outer wall. The walls were wide enough to hold catapults of all sizes and varieties, so that attackers would be assailed with boulders, spears and stones.

Castles were built with both outer and inner walls. Even if the attackers succeeded in breeching the outer one they would find themselves facing the inner one, which was usually just as strong and high as the outer. Sandwiched between the two, with defenders shooting at them from above, they found themselves in what was called in World War I "no man's land," and today is called a "killing field." They were often butchered by the thousands.

Adding to a castle's impregnability was its location. They were usually built on top of hills or rocky outcroppings, with terrain that was hard to climb. Thus nature lent its own defenses to those devised by the builders.

Despite these difficulties, armies frequently had to defeat castles. They were usually home to large numbers of enemy forces, as well as the chief or king of the territory as well as his gold, jewels, and other wealth. Thus medieval warriors developed numerous ways of assaulting castles.

Bribery was often successful. Every castle had secret entrances called "sally ports" from which agents of the king could leave to deliver messages or spy on the enemy. It was often possible to make contact with someone inside the walls who knew where these ports were and would make a deal to leave them open. As night fell the attackers entered through them and took over while most inside the castle were asleep.

Another tactic was simple negotiation. The commander of the attacking army would alternately use threats and promises of mercy to persuade the defenders to give up.

Sometimes they would take the heads of captured enemies and toss them over the walls, to show the inhabitants what would happen if they didn't give up. Then they would promise to spare the occupants' lives if they simply opened the gates and let them in.

Still another technique was surrounding the castle and letting no one in or out. With supplies unable to reach the castles, those inside its walls would often face famine and thirst until at last they gave up. Castle builders anticipated this, though, and usually stocked them with months' worth of food, fresh water and other provisions. Often it was the attackers who would succumb to hunger and thirst, while those inside the walls enjoyed plentiful supplies.

If all these tactics failed, then there was only one way to bring down a castle, and that was to lay siege to it. For this purpose catapults were constructed on site that could keep up a constant barrage against the stone walls. Day and night they would hurl boulders towards the fortifications, while the defenders responded with their own catapults as well as arrow fire. Meanwhile tunnelers would start to dig out the foundations underneath the walls, making them unstable and more vulnerable to assault. Those in the castle would counter by digging their own tunnels. There are accounts of passageways from both sides linking, and soldiers fighting deadly underground battles.

Sometimes the attackers' catapults and tunnels were unable to damage the walls. It was a common sight for medieval defenders to take out their handkerchiefs and dust the spot where a stone had just bounced off their castle, as a way to mock the assaulters.

On other occasions, though, the artillery did its job. First a crack would appear, and then it would spread as more stones were hurled against it, and then finally holes would appear. The attackers would rush forward with picks to enlarge the openings, and then the infantry would charge in.

The battle would turn to hand-to-hand fighting at this point. Ancient warfare was almost always a bloody, horrific affair because of its face-to-face nature.

Since their invention in ancient times up until the Middle Ages, most catapults were powered by elastic cords, but this technology had its limitations. When it rained, the cords would go slack and become useless.

This problem was solved by the Chinese. In the 500s they developed a new form of catapult that used counter weights to propel the ammunition instead of coiled springs. This technology gradually spread to Europe, and the first major advance in artillery technology in fifteen hundred years, the trebuchet, was born. An example is shown below:

Figure 1-3

To understand how this works, picture a seesaw.

The board stays perfectly balanced as long as the weight on each end is equal.

Now take the fulcrum (the triangle the base rests on) and move it closer to one end of the board. Then drop a heavy weight on the short end. This is what will happen:

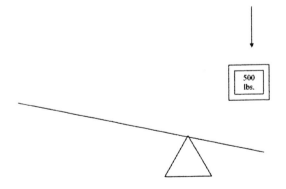

Figure 1-4

Get the idea? On one end of the throwing arm is a giant bucket filled with rocks, pieces of metal, etc. On the other end is a large sling that could hold stones weighing well over a hundred pounds. When fired the arm would spring up in a great, looping arc, sending the load flying through the air and crashing against the distant fortification.

Figure 1-5

This catapult had numerous advantages over the old spring powered ones. Since weight is a constant, it could hit the same spot over and over, making the process of breaking down castle walls much more efficient. Also firepower was limited only by the size of the trebuchet. Monster ones were built throughout medieval times. Perhaps the most formidable was Ludgar the War Wolf, built by King Edward to besiege

Stirling Castle in Scotland in 1304. Capable of tossing three hundred pound stones, it shattered a wall of the castle with its first round.

This was the apex of catapult use. Over the next two hundred years the use of them would wane and finally disappear. The cause: a fiery, mysterious black powder from China. It would change everything.

The Gunpowder Revolution

In the 9th century A.D. Chinese alchemists mixed together saltpeter, charcoal and sulfur during an experiment. The result was a fine gray mixture that exploded on contact with heat or flame. It also produced copious amounts of superheated gas. They began to use it in fireworks and pyrotechnic displays. They also made limited military use of it in crude cannons, but never fully developed its potential.

Knowledge of how to make the powder passed in the 1300s from the Mongols to Europeans, who were quicker than their eastern counterparts to see its potential as a weapon. They first used it as a propellant for cannon-launched stones. The first gunpowder-based artillery pieces were crude, resembling a bowling pin. The weapon was packed with powder and the opening on the narrow end was plugged with a metal arrow. The powder was ignited by holding a red-hot wire to the touch hole in the rear. In terms of power it was slightly stronger than a crossbow and horribly inaccurate.

Experiments continued, though. The powder itself was vastly improved by adding water or urine to the mix, then drying it out. This improved its stability and the force of its explosion. Then improvements in metallurgy allowed the building of stronger and more reliable cannons. By the end of the 14th century wrought-iron cannons were firing 450 pound balls with more force and distance than the strongest catapult.

The last successful use of a trebuchet occurred in 1480, when Greek defenders used one to silence the cannons of the attacking Turks. But by then the handwriting was on the wall. The catapult's days were numbered.

Word of the new gunpowder weapons was spreading among the European nobility. Soon it became the "in" thing for a nobleman to equip his soldiers with them. The noise and smoke they produced had a potent psychological effect on the enemy, and continuing improvements made them cheaper and safer to use. By 1500, mechanical artillery in all forms had virtually disappeared from Europe.

The final recorded military use of a catapult was in 1521, when Cortez was fighting the Aztecs. Ammunition for the Spanish cannons was running low, and an ambitious young soldier came up with the idea of building a trebuchet. Unfortunately his engineering knowledge was less than perfect, and the first stone fired went straight up in the air, and then landed on the weapon itself, destroying it. It was a sign of the times. Mechanical artillery, which had served armies faithfully for two millennia, was out.

The Catapult is Reborn

In 1986 a group of men were standing around a blacksmith shop in Delaware arguing over who could toss an anvil the furthest. For unknown reasons the discussion changed from throwing anvils to pumpkins, and hand tossing was abandoned in favor of mechanical throwing devices.

In early winter of that year the men gathered in a nearby field with their homemade catapults. One inventor brought a contraption cobbled together from old ropes, tubes and pulleys. Another brought a device powered by garage and auto springs. By day's end one team stood victorious, having thrown a pumpkin 128 feet with their machine.

From that friendly competition was born the greatest catapult event in modern times, the annual Punkin Chunkin contest, held in November of each year, in Forest Grove, Oregon. Thousands of people from across the country gather to watch inventors match catapults, trebuchets, air cannons and other devices against each other. The goal is to see whose device can chunk a ten to twelve pound pumpkin the furthest. Not only individuals but engineering groups, high school science clubs, Boy Scout troops and even major corporations vie for the championship and bragging rights.

The catapults compete in a class of their own. The current record is held by the team that built Hypertension, a metal monster powered by huge industrial springs. In 2004 it tossed a twelve pound pumpkin 2,111 feet (704 yards). The champion trebuchet, Yankee Siege, tossed one of the same weight 1,394 feet (465 yards).

This event is a helluva lot of fun. Groups gather the day before the competition to build bonfires, listen to live music, eat good food, and socialize. Some strong friendships have been formed among the competitors as well as several fierce rivalries. You can learn more about this great event by visiting www.punkinchunkin.com.

A small group of southerners, myself included, has a similar event in the planning stages, one that will take place in summer. Watermelons will be the projectiles of choice. If all goes well you'll be reading more about it in the third edition of this book. Other competitions already occur in the Midwest.

Punkin Chunkin is the best known example of the interest modern people are taking in catapults, but it is by no means the only one. In 2000 the public television show Nova sponsored a group of inventors in Scotland. Their job was to recreate the monster trebuchet that King Edward used to defeat the Scots at Stirling Castle. The final version was enormous, with a 13,000 pound throwing arm. After much trial and error it was able to fire 250 pound stones accurately over 200 yards at a speed of 120 miles an hour.

A quick search of eBay under the keyword "catapult" will reveal dozens of plans, models and finished versions of toy catapults. There are a plethora of web sites devoted exclusively to the subject. Centuries after being dismissed from the battlefield, catapults have become a subject of intense interest among a wide variety of people.

It's not hard to understand why. There is something both primal and exhilarating about something that can toss big rocks across great distances. It appeals to the inner child in all of us.

At the same time, if knowledge of metallurgy, ballistics and the countless other disciplines necessary to build modern artillery should ever be lost, then knowing how to build these machines could come in handy. Wars will continue, and those with superior technology will continue to win them. This was as true during the Roman Empire as it is today. So, whether your interest in mechanical artillery is just for fun or motivated by a desire to survive, I welcome you aboard.

Chapter Two
Build a Base

Every construction project needs a good foundation, and a catapult is no exception. In this section we'll build a base that will serve as the platform for three different weapons. It is made of wood and is sturdy but lightweight. Building it should take no more than a few hours of work.

These are the materials you will need:

- *One wooden pallet* – the kind that goods are shipped on, in decent shape. This can be had for free or at very low cost from store owners, salvage yards, or advertised in local shoppers. You can also snatch one for free from nearly any retail dumpster. I found mine at the landfill.
- *Seven – 8 foot 2"x 4"s* – get treated ones if you can. Make sure they're straight and aren't full of knots. It always pays to buy the highest grade of lumber you can afford.
- *One – 10 foot 2"x 6"*
- *Lots of 3" screws*, a power drill with screw driving tips, a saw (circular or hand), a pair of saw horses, assorted hand tools.
- *One – piece of pipe*, 1.5" in diameter and at least four inches longer than the width of the pallet.

Figure 2-1

Okay! First off, place the pallet on saw horses, then cut a 2 foot length of 2″ x 4″, line it up flush with the front of the pallet, then screw it to the pallet. Refer to Figure 2-2.

Figure 2-2

Next, place the 2″ x 6″ flush against the piece of 2″ x 4″ you just screwed in. This is to provide space for the arms that will be attached later. Take the remaining six foot length of 2″ x 4″, place it flush against the other side of the 2″ x 6″, and then screw it in along the length of pallet. Refer to Figure 2-3.

Figure 2-3

Do the same for the other side of the pallet. At this point the project should look like Figure 2-4 from the rear.

Figure 2-4

Remove the 2″ x 6″ spacer. Next, measure the distance between the 2″ x 4″s, cut another piece of 2″ x 4″ that length, and screw it into the rear of the base as shown in Figure 2-5.

Figure 2-5

Also, measure the length from the end of the pallet to the ends of the 2″ x 4″s. Cut a piece of 2″ x 4″ that length and insert it in the middle as shown in Figure 2-6.

Figure 2-6

Now we're going to cut and attach the arms that will support the various weapons.

Cut two pieces of 2″ x 6″ lumber 4 feet 3.5″ long. Drill a 1.5″ hole in each, centered and 2″ from the end of each. Then, in the spaces you left earlier, line the bottoms of the 2″ x 6″s up with the bottoms of 2″ x 4″s that are screwed to the pallet. Make sure they're at a 90 degree angle. Screw them into place using 3″ wood screws. Refer to Figure 2-7.

Figure 2-7

Are we having fun yet?

Now we're going to brace those support arms. Cut an 8′ 2″ x 4″ in half and use the pieces to brace the support arms as shown in Figure 2-8.

Figure 2-8

Almost there! All that's left is to insert the 1.5″ piece of metal pipe into the holes we drilled into the support arms. See Figure 2-9. If they match what you've built then you've done it right.

Figure 2-9

As mentioned before, this base will be the foundation of the three weapons we will build. The first will most closely resemble the device people think of when they hear the word "catapult." So let's flip the page and learn how to build an onager.

Chapter Three
Build an Onager

Figure 3-1

    This is one of the most ancient catapult designs, and it was used extensively by both the Greeks and Romans. Although the drawing shows a "scoop" mounted on the end of the throwing arm, it was much more common for it to have a sling instead. These weapons were the "atom bombs" of their day, and were used with devastating effect against both personnel and fortifications.

In modern times there have been many attempts to build "authentic" versions of these devices, but the spring mechanism is always a stumbling block. The ancients used elastic cords made of a combination of human hair and animal sinew, which they wrapped around the throwing arms to give them the necessary "spring."

The exact way this was done has been lost in history, and all efforts to replicate it have ended in failure. So for our purposes we will dispense with the ancient ways of propelling the shot, using instead a very modern substitute: a garage door spring.

As we have already built the base, in this section we'll see how to construct the throwing arm, sling, and trigger mechanism. This same arm will also be used for our next project, the trebuchet. The difference is that it will use counterweights to toss the arm rather than a spring.

To build the onager's throwing arm, we will need:

- *One 10 foot 2"x 4",* preferably pressure treated (or a 2" x 6", depending on spring strength; see below).
- *One 8 foot 2"x 6",* again preferably pressure treated.
- *One garage door spring.* These are sold at home improvement warehouses such as Lowe's and Home Depot. They range in size and strength, from 70 pounds to 160 pounds. For this project we'll use a 100 pound spring. A stronger spring will work just as well, but if you use one I strongly recommend using a 10 foot 2" x 6" rather than the 10 foot 2" x 4" listed above, because of higher stresses on the lumber.
- *One 2 foot long bungee cord* with hooks on either end.
- *Two – 6" long eye bolts,* with eyes wider in diameter than the ends of the spring.

- *Two – 3″ long eye bolts* with eyes wide enough for the hooks on the bungee cord to pass through.
- *About fifteen feet of strong, heavy cord;* light rope can work if it's not stiff.
- *One heavy door or gate hinge*
- *One – 4 foot piece of 2″ x 4″*
- *Assorted long bolts or screws*
- *One – scrap piece of 1″ x 4″,* at least 4 inches long
- *One – 1 foot by 3 foot piece of heavy canvas,* denim or leather for the sling.

Step One: Cut the 2″ x 6″ in half. Place pieces on either side of the 10 foot 2″ x 4″. Make sure bottoms of all three boards are flush and that the 2″ x 4″ is centered equal lengths from edges of 2″ x 6″s. Bolt or screw all three pieces of wood together. See Figures 3-2 and Figure 3-3.

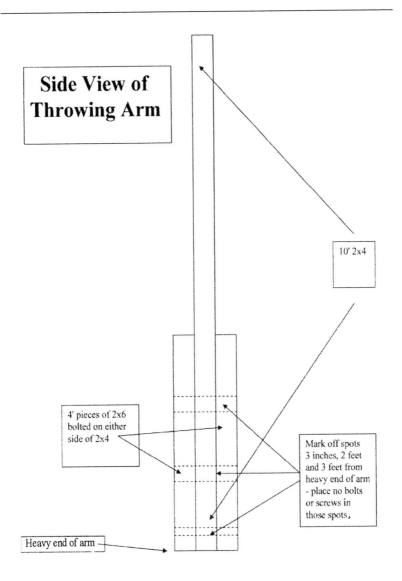

Figure 3-2

Figure 3-3

Step Two: Now we're going to make some holes. Drill a 1.5″ hole, centered and 3 inches from the heavy end of the throwing arm. Drill another 2.5 feet from the end and another 3.5 feet from the end. Refer to photos.

Figure 3-4

Step Three: Run metal pipe on base through the hole that is 3.5 feet from end of throwing arm. Arm will now rotate on the pipe as in Figure 3-5.

Figure 3-5

Step Four: Place the spring end against the bottom of the
throwing arm and secure in place by screwing in an eye bolt.
Drill a pilot hole in the bottom of the 2″ x 4″ so the eye bolt
will screw in easily. See Figure 3-6.

Figure 3-6

Step Five: Now we're going to build the trigger device. When the throwing arm is lowered it will automatically cock the trigger in place. The trigger will keep the arm from launching until you decide to fire it.

First, screw one side of the hinge onto the bottom of the 4 foot length of 2″ x 4″. Then screw the other side onto the length of 2″ x 4″ running down the middle of the base. See Figures 3-7 and 3-8.

Figure 3-7

Figure 3-8

Nail scrap pieces of 2″ x 4″ or 2″ x 6″ over the side of the hinge screwed into the 2″ x 4″; refer again to Figure 3-8; they're meant to keep the arm from flipping over to the left. Now screw a 3 inch eye bolt into the side of the 2″ x 4″ about

3 feet up. Screw another one into the base as shown in Figure 3-8. Hook the bungee cord through these eye bolts. Finally take a scrap piece of 1″ x 4″, cut a slant in it, and screw it to top of the trigger four foot 2″ x 4″; refer to Figures 3-7 and 3-8.

This completes the trigger arm. It works as shown on page 41:

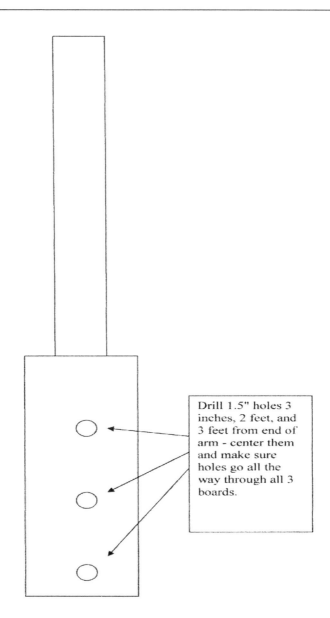

Drill 1.5" holes 3 inches, 2 feet, and 3 feet from end of arm - center them and make sure holes go all the way through all 3 boards.

Figure 3-9

Step Six: Now we're going to make the sling. First cut holes in each corner of the piece of heavy cloth as in Figure 3-10.

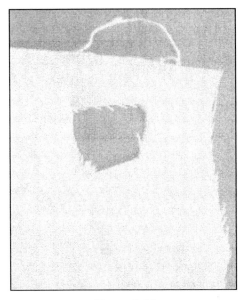

Figure 3-10

Step Seven: Hang a piece of heavy cord or light rope over the light end of the throwing arm about 1 foot from the end, so that approximately one foot of cord hangs from each side of the arm; secure on top with a fence staple. See Figure 3-11.

Figure 3-11

Step Eight: Hang another piece the same length just in front of first one, but let it hang free. Don't secure it with fence staple. See Figure 3-12.

Figure 3-12

Step Nine: Tie the rope ends through each hole in sling cloth as in Figures 3-13 and 3-14.

Figure 3-13

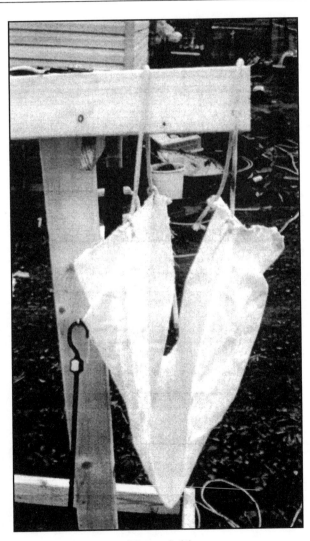

Figure 3-14

Step Ten: Take a deep breath and get a cold drink; we're almost done! Now we want to connect the free end of the spring to the base. To do so, secure it to the base with the remaining eye bolt as in Figure 3-15.

Figure 3-15

Make sure the eye bolt goes deep into both 2″ x 4″s for security.

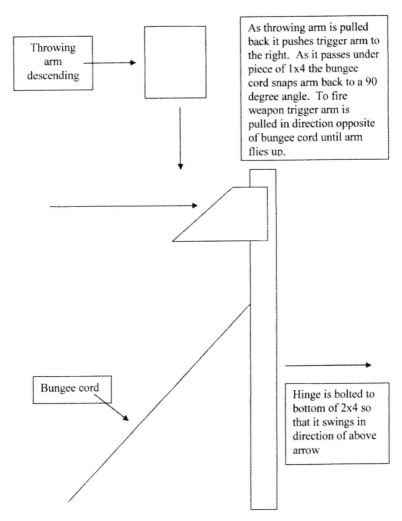

As throwing arm is pulled back it pushes trigger arm to the right. As it passes under piece of 1x4 the bungee cord snaps arm back to a 90 degree angle. To fire weapon trigger arm is pulled in direction opposite of bungee cord until arm flies up.

Throwing arm descending

Bungee cord

Hinge is bolted to bottom of 2x4 so that it swings in direction of above arrow

Figure 3-16

Step Eleven: Lower the arm into firing position. This can be dangerous to do by hand. I throw a rope around the top of the arm just below the sling, loop it around the arm and pull it down until the trigger arm locks it in place. You may want to use a winching system like the one we'll look at when we build the ballista.

Now see Figure 3-17 for what the weapon should look like now.

Figure 3-17

Place your ammo in the center of the pouch. Full cans of cheap soda make great ammunition. So do standard sized mortar bricks, small chunks of wood, or pop bottles. Any of these will likely be tossed about a hundred yards with a one hundred pound spring.

At this point the weapon is ready to fire. To do so, pull the trigger arm in the direction opposite the bungee cord. You can do this by hand or loop some cord around the arm and pull it.

At no time let any part of your body get in the path of the throwing arm! It comes up very fast and it will hurt or kill you if it strikes you!

You may find that the frame slides towards you as you pull the trigger arm back. Use your foot to hold it in place if it does. Then let that arm fly. WOOSH! It shoots upward, the sling deploys its charge, and it flies across the landscape. Make sure there's nothing in front of the onager you don't want to hit.

This thing is a helluva lot of fun, and safe as long as common sense is used. After firing a few times check the frame to make sure it's holding up and the eye bolts that hold the spring in place aren't coming loose. This is a sensible precaution, but if you've built well then you should have no worries. Have fun!

Figure 3-18

Chapter Four
Build a Trebuchet

In the last section we saw how to build an onager, a weapon that uses spring power. Now we're going to build a modern day version of the catapult below:

Trebuchets threw a variety of ammunition — in this case a dead horse.

Figure 4-1

As we discussed earlier, the trebuchet uses a heavy counterweight on the short end of the throwing arm. For our purposes I chose to use standard weightlifting disks. Why? Well, first of all they're cheap. You can buy a hundred pounds or more at Wal-Mart for less than thirty bucks. Second, they're durable. Third, they're easy to get on and off the throwing arm.

The big advantage of the trebuchet is that you can adjust its range simply by adding or taking away weight, while with the onager you are stuck with whatever throwing power the spring generates. You could, of course, change out the springs, alternating stronger and weaker ones. But that would be a time consuming process.

Changing the throwing power can come in handy if you are shooting your trebuchet in, say, your backyard. The last thing you want it to do is chunk a rock onto your neighbor's azaleas. (Then again, maybe that's the first thing you want.) In any event, having control over the weapon's range can be a big advantage.

Okay, ready? Here we go.

Step One: If you have already attached the onager spring to the throwing arm we built in the last chapter, then remove it now. Screw out the eye bolts that hold it to the arm as well as to the base. Inserting a long screwdriver through the eye then twisting it makes this much easier and faster.

Step Two: Pull the throwing arm off of the pipe it rotates on, then put it back on, this time through the middle hole you drilled, the one that is 2.5 feet from the heavy end.

Figure 4-2

Step Three: Take a heavy piece of chain, loop it through the bottom hole, slide the weights onto it as well, then use either heavy cord or a padlock to secure the chain together in a closed loop.

Figure 4-3

That's all the modifications that are needed! The trebuchet operates just like the onager, except for weight providing the tossing force. How much weight should you use? I got ranges of about fifty yards tossing small chunks of wood with about 120 pounds of weight. I would start with, say, fifty or sixty pounds if I were you, then increase the weight until the desired range is achieved.

Caution: The center board in the throwing arm should be upgraded from a 2"x 4" to either a 2" x 6" or 4" x 4" if you are going to be using more than 120 pounds of weights. Wood should never be forced to handle more stress than it was designed for.

Happy bombarding.

Chapter Five
Build a Ballista

Figure 5-1

Of all the projects in this book this one is my favorite. There's nothing like seeing the twin springs shoot forward and launch a piece of wood or metal-tipped bolt into the air. Maybe it's the mental image of the spear splitting my boss in two that makes it such fun; I'm not sure.

In ancient times the ballista was a fearsome weapon. The Romans used them with deadly efficiency in both warfare and crowd control. Basically an oversized crossbow, its giant arrows could tear through four to five men at a time. Beautiful!

As with the trebuchet and onager, this weapon uses the base we built in Chapter One. Though its elevation can be changed at will, I strongly recommend firing it from the position shown in the photos. It gets the best range that way.

Ready to start building? Okay then, let's go!

First the materials. This is what you will need:

- *One – 8 foot 2"x 6"*
- *One – 8 foot 4"x 4"*
- *One – 3 foot length of 4"x 4"*
- *Two garage door springs*. I used 70 pound springs for mine, but the frame can handle any made up to 160 pounds. Remember: the stronger the spring the farther it will shoot.
- *Four – 6" eye bolts*; the eyes must be wider in diameter than the ends of the springs. Refer back to the throwing arm for the onager.
- *One – 8 foot length of 1"x 2" lumber*. Make sure it's very straight.
- *A foot or so of heavy cord or light rope*.
- *One – S-hook*, about 3" to 4" long.
- *One – 8" or longer metal spike*. A smooth piece of pipe no more than $3/8"$ in diameter and 8" long will do as well. So will a long screwdriver.
- *One hand-operated winch*, plus the wire cord it will use to pull things. My winch is rated at 600 pounds.
- *One turnbuckle*, about 5"-6" long.

- ***Wood screws*** up to 3″ long, plus the basic tools we used earlier.

Step One: Place the 4″ x 4″ and 2″ x 6″ on the saw horses as shown in Figure 5-2.

Figure 5-2

Step Two: Place the 2″ x 6″ on top of the 4″ x 4″, with one foot of the 2″ x 6″ extending past the end of the 4″ x 4″. See Figure 5-3.

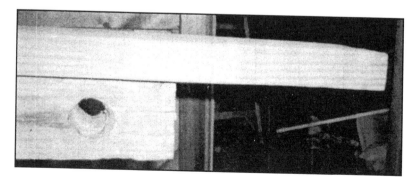

Figure 5-3

Step Three: Using 3″ wood screws, screw the 2″ x 6″ onto the 4″ x 4″. Make sure you countersink the screws into the 2″ x 6″.

Step Four: Center the three foot length of 4″ x 4″ against the end of the 8 foot 4″ x 4″, under the 2″ x 6″. See Figures 5-4, 5-5, and 5-6.

Figure 5-4

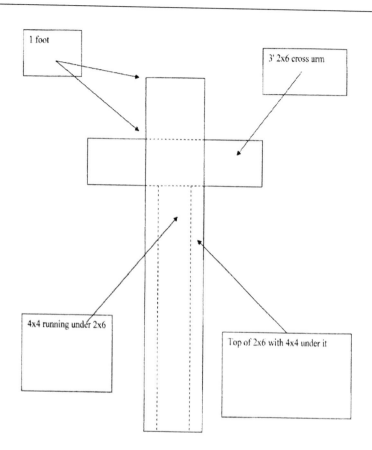

1 foot

3' 2x6 cross arm

4x4 running under 2x6

Top of 2x6 with 4x4 under it

TOP VIEW

Figure 5-5

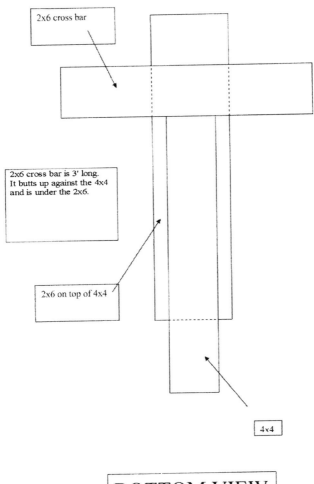

2x6 cross bar

2x6 cross bar is 3' long.
It butts up against the 4x4
and is under the 2x6.

2x6 on top of 4x4

4x4

BOTTOM VIEW

Figure 5-6

Step Five: Center the ends of the springs about 3″ from the ends of the 3-foot cross bar. Secure the springs to the cross bar with the eye bolts. Tie the other ends of the springs together with heavy cord, leaving a length of about 3″ between them. Run cords through one end of the turnbuckle. See photos and drawings.

Figure 5-7

Figure 5-8

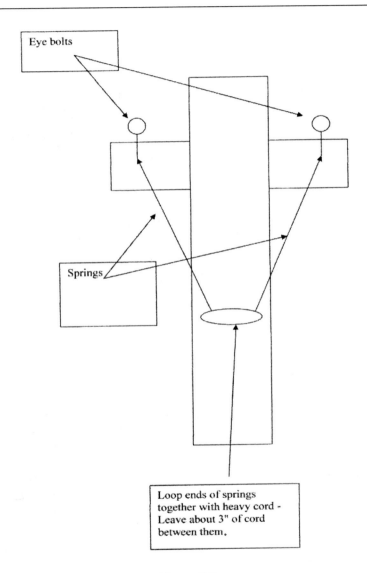

Eye bolts

Springs

Loop ends of springs
together with heavy cord -
Leave about 3" of cord
between them.

Figure 5-9

Step Six: Bolt the winch onto the end of the 2" x 6". Unwind its pulling cord and hook the S-hook onto the end. See Figure 5-10.

Figure 5-10

Step Seven: Cut the 1" x 2" in half. Place on the 2" x 6", about 4" in front of the winch. Measure the distance in between them; it should be just slightly over an inch and a half. Slide a scrap piece of 2" x 4" or 2" x 6" between them. It should slide easily but not loosely. Screw down the 1" x 2"s, with the 2-inch end flush against the 2" x 6". See Figures 5-11 and 5-12.

Figure 5-11

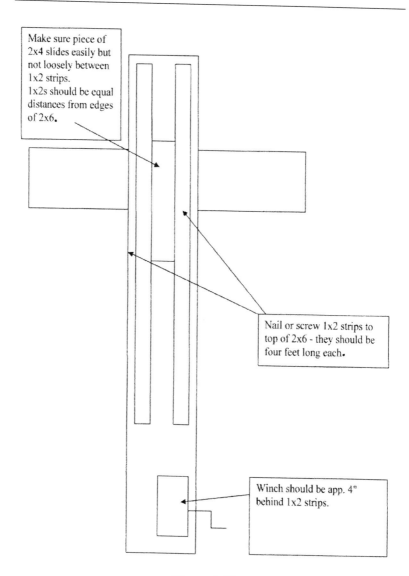

Make sure piece of 2x4 slides easily but not loosely between 1x2 strips.
1x2s should be equal distances from edges of 2x6.

Nail or screw 1x2 strips to top of 2x6 - they should be four feet long each.

Winch should be app. 4" behind 1x2 strips.

Figure 5-12

Step Eight: Screw 2 eye bolts into the 2″ x 6″, a few inches in front of the winch. Each should be about 1″ from the edge of the 2″ x 6″. See Figures 5-13 and 5-14.

Figure 5-13

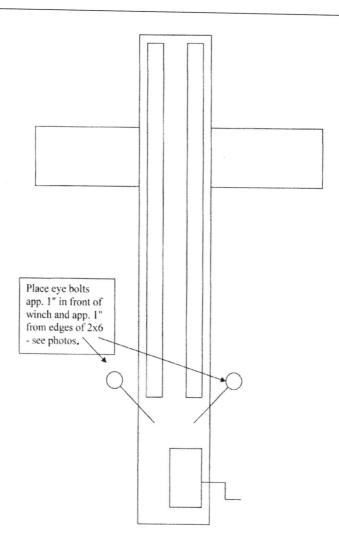

Place eye bolts app. 1" in front of winch and app. 1" from edges of 2x6 - see photos.

Figure 5-14

Step Nine: Drill a 1½" hole on the end of the 8 foot 4" x 4" just before the crossbar. This hole will need to slide easily on and off the pipe on the base, so wobble the wood bit a little as

you drill the hole. This will make it slightly larger than 1½".
See Figure 5-15.

Figure 5-15

Step Ten: Now we're ready for some fun. Slide the end of
the ballista onto the pipe as shown in Figure 5-16.

Figure 5-16

Then crank the cord backwards until the hole in the turnbuckle lines up with the holes in the eye bolts that are just in front of the winch. See Figures 5-17 and 5-18.

Figure 5-17

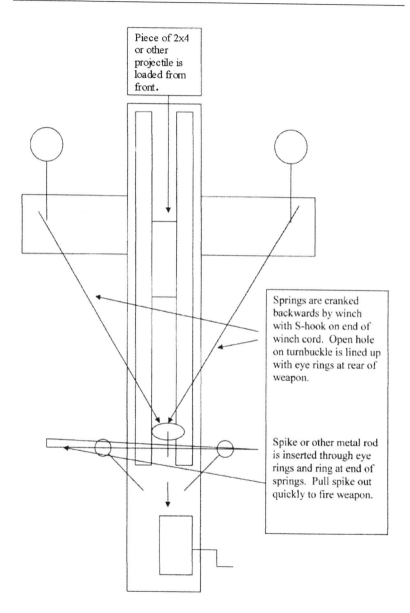

Piece of 2x4 or other projectile is loaded from front.

Springs are cranked backwards by winch with S-hook on end of winch cord. Open hole on turnbuckle is lined up with eye rings at rear of weapon.

Spike or other metal rod is inserted through eye rings and ring at end of springs. Pull spike out quickly to fire weapon.

Figure 5-18

Slip the metal spike or pipe through the eye bolts and the turnbuckle hole as shown in Figure 5-19, then release the pressure on the winch and remove the S-hook. Then put your choice of ammo between the 1" x 2"s; I recommend a short piece of 2" x 4" for your first shot, no more than 6" long.

Figure 5-19

The weapon is now ready to fire. To do so, yank the spike or whatever you slipped through the eyebolts out quickly. You may want to grease the insides of the eye bolts to make this easier.

WOOSH! The springs fly forward, the cord holding them together hits the projectile, and it goes flying through the air. Neat-o!

As mentioned before, this weapon was originally used to shoot large metal-tipped spears through human flesh. Since most readers of this book probably don't want to commit homicide I suggest using small lengths of 2″ x 4″ lumber instead. However, for those interested in this device's lethal potential, I invite you to join me in the "Beyond Fun and Games" chapter, which is coming up next. There you'll see a homemade spear with very interesting possibilities.

Have fun — and don't kill yourself in the process.

Figure 5-20

Chapter Six
Beyond Fun and Games

Most of this book has been all about fun and games. I haven't been writing for those who are interested in building onagers, trebuchets, etc. for military purposes. In this section that will change.

Many people are concerned that civilization is on the verge of major trouble, if not outright collapse. Whether it's caused by economic instability, government oppression, terrorism, ecological calamity, or what have you, they are preparing for a major crisis.

If you are of that mindset then the rest of this book is for you. We're going to look at how mechanical artillery can be used in both offensive and defensive scenarios. We'll explore how to build catapults with strong destructive potentials. And I'll offer my insights into their strengths and weaknesses.

Know thy Limitations

First off, realize this: catapults haven't been used in battle since the early 1500s, and that's not likely to change. If you dream of creating a sanctuary and using catapults to counter Big Brother's cannons, tanks, and aircraft, forget it. You may as well shoot spitballs at them. You'll be wiped out quicker than you can say New World Order.

That doesn't mean that there aren't scenarios where these weapons could come in handy. The fact is, modern military systems have an Achilles heel of their own: their dependence on technical support and reliable logistics to keep them working. If our modern infrastructure should be disrupted, then catapults could become the best artillery available.

It wasn't just the discovery of gunpowder that led to modern weapons. Truth is, the early black powders were inefficient and unreliable. The ingredients would separate during transport. They often fizzled out before firing a shot. Other times they were packed too tightly and the cannon just blew up in the faces of its crew.

It was advances in metallurgy, such as the development of stronger iron and the ability to bore riflings into barrels, that finally made the cannon the artillery piece of choice. This didn't occur until well into the 1700s.

Before that, gunpowder weapons were often just noisy, inaccurate, and unreliable noisemakers. In fact, up until the 19th century, many military authorities favored abandoning cannons altogether in favor of catapults. Accuracy, reliability and simplicity were all factors in their favor.

Imagine a disaster that disrupts our national transportation system. The country is in chaos. Army units worldwide are suffering crucial supply shortages. Sophisticated weapons systems sit idle because of technical problems that can't be fixed. Even cartridges are precious commodities. In such a situation, a group armed with weapons that can fire metal-tipped bolts over a hundred miles an hour and toss fifty pound rocks a couple hundred yards could be powerful indeed.

These weapons can be built with muscle power and a few basic tools, out of materials available in any junkyard. Familiarity with some basic physics and wood-joining techniques, plus a strong back, are all one needs to make his own.

Let's imagine a scenario in which they would be useful. Visualize this: a few days ago the sun bathed the earth in powerful solar flares never before seen. The result was the destruction of almost every electronic device on the planet. Radios, TVs, computers, telephones, wireless communications, even most cars and trucks are useless piles of junk.

Silence descends over the planet, followed swiftly by chaos as riots break out in the major cities. Food supplies disappear, and urbanites who couldn't live a week without their ATM cards and PCs are starving. In desperation they pour out into the countryside.

I am familiar with the city of Atlanta, as well as the terrain that surrounds it, so I'm going to focus our imaginary catastrophe on this part of the world. There is a rag-tag horde of looters making its way up the I-85 northern corridor from the metro area. They are raiding farms and small towns, taking not only food, but tools, guns, jewelry, and anything else of value from helpless citizens.

As they approach the mountains, a collection of rednecks, hillbillies, blue-collar types, and agrarians band together for common defense. One of them has a copy of a book entitled **Backyard Catapults: How to Build Your Own**. The group's leaders study it. Then they set about cannibalizing springs from cars and factories, chopping down trees to build massive wooden frames, making slings and finding large rocks for ammunition.

They erect barriers cross the abandoned interstate and position catapults at each one. They are also armed with their own pistols, rifles, and shotguns, as well as hunting bows and even slingshots.

Two days later they see the approaching looters. They've been experimenting with their new artillery and know its range. They fire some warning shots but the throng of rioters keeps coming.

They hold their fire until the front of the mob is within two hundred yards of them. Then they let loose. A hail of boulders rains down on the invaders, followed by giant spears that pierce four or five of them at a time. The "woosh!" of trebuchets is heard as old auto parts, stones, nails, tacks, Molotov cocktails and other nasty things pour down on the attackers.

Most of the looters flee in panic. The few that keep coming are picked off by small arms fire. The rural community is saved by guts, teamwork, and reliance on ancient technology.

Later the author of the catapult book is located. The grateful people who were saved by his writings crown him philosopher-king. Under his wise leadership, a benevolent empire spreads across the earth, and a golden age of peace and prosperity begins.

Okay, the last paragraph was a bit far-fetched, but the rest is well within the range of possibility. So let's see just how such a victory could be pulled off.

Bigger is Better

Four garage springs are better than one for tossing a stone an appreciable distance. A thousand pounds of counterweight will send that homemade grenade further than a hundred pounds will. By using heavier lumber than what I did, you can create frames that will handle the accompanying stresses of adding more force to your creations. The ancients attained ranges of up to 450 yards with their catapults. We're talking four and a half football fields laid end to end. That's not bad.

If an enemy group was approaching your territory *en masse*, then concentrated fire from several catapults could do some serious damage, possibly halting their advance. At the very least it could thin their ranks considerably. Even one such weapon could give them pause.

What would such a super-catapult look like? Look at the pictures of the classic machines in this book. Also, I am going to give you a design for a weapon, which currently exists only in my mind. Size, cost, and range considerations have kept me from actually building it. However, if I can find someone with a "back 40," and if negotiations over the advance for this book go the author's way, then it may soon become a reality. Check it out:

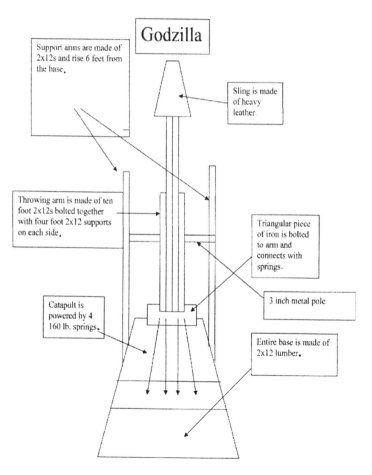

Figure 6-1

Feel free to tackle the project if you like. And write to me in care of Loompanics Unlimited and tell me how it went. Send pictures.

Final Thoughts

Well, here we are at the end. I hope you've enjoyed the ride. And now that it's over the rest is up to you. Take what I've said in this book and put it to use. Build your own ballistas, onagers, and trebuchets. Start out making them like I did. But don't stop there. Surpass me. Build them bigger and better and stronger than mine. This book is just a starting point. Use it to whet your imagination, to dream of things not yet built, things that can be, if only you try.

Wherever your interest in catapults takes you, I wish you all the best. Thanks for reading the book. Excelsior!

Bill Wilson
May 2005

Resources

www.stormthewalls.dhs.org: Great site for further research. Lots of plans, history, and links.

www.trebuchet.com: This is an absolutely fantastic site. It features message boards, plans, and photos of weapons others have built.

www.punkinchunkin.com: Has information on the annual Punkin Chunkin national festival, where catapult enthusiasts gather to launch pumpkins across a huge field and to show off their inventions. Great fun! Lots of links also.

To find out more about the annual Punkin Chunkin, you can write to World Championship Punkin Chunkin Association, PO Box 217, Nassau, DE 19969 or call them at 302-684-8196.

Lastly, feel free to write to me in care of Loompanics Unlimited, PO Box 1197, Port Townsend, WA 98368, if you have any questions or comments. Best of Luck!

YOU WILL ALSO WANT TO READ:

☐ **19246 THE NEW BULLWHIP BOOK, by Andrew Conway.** Have you ever looked at a person with the bullwhip on the movie screen and thought, *"Hmmmm, I wonder if I could do that?" Yes, you can.* This profusely illustrated book introduces you to the three basic cracks and step-by-step instructions on how to master those cracks and variations of them. So get cracking, and get your copy today. *2005, 8½ x 11, 128 pp, illustrated, soft cover. $12.95.*

☐ **19103 THE SLING, For Sport & Survival, by Cliff Savage.** A complete, illustrated guide to making and using a sling — the ancient weapon David used to kill Goliath. Slings are silent, accurate, and deadly. They are more powerful than a bow, and ammunition is free. Easily improvised and highly portable, they are increasingly used in urban guerrilla warfare. Step-by-step illustrated slinging stances, construction techniques, and ammunition ideas highlight this book. It is highly recommended for all survivalists and weapons enthusiasts. *1990, 5½ x 8½, 84 pp, soft cover. $8.95.*

☐ **19216 THE SCOURGE OF THE DARK CONTINENT: The Martial Use of the African Sjambok, by James Loriega and a Foreword by James Keating.** The sjambok is one of the most versatile and effective of all flexible weapons, having been used for centuries in Africa. The author has written the first book-length treatment of the defensive use of the sjambok. Loriega, a well-known and respected martial arts expert, covers every aspect of the sjambok. In illustrated detail, Loriega explains the basic combat stances, whipping methods, striking methods, as well as which targets are best for each method, and much more. *1999, 5½ x 8½, 143 pp, illustrated, soft cover. $8.95.*

☐ **32060 DAVID'S TOOL KIT; A Citizen's Guide to Taking Out Big Brother's Heavy Weapons, by Ragnar Benson.** What do you do when faced with the overwhelming firepower of ruthless authority? Fight back, that's what. Ragnar Benson provides citizen defenders with the information they need to mount a successful campaign against overwhelming odds... and win! Brief histories of armed resistance and tank warfare are included. This may be the most essential self-defense book ever written! *1996, 5½ x 8½, 217 pp, illustrated, soft cover. $16.95.*

☐ **32039 NIGHT MOVEMENTS, Translated from the Japanese.** This rare translation of a Japanese military text is generally regarded as the finest study of night fighting ever written. Used to train snipers, scouts and saboteurs in World War I, it has become one of the classic training manuals for insurgents all over the world. Covered are: psychology; silence; dress; vision; hearing; shooting; demolition; battles; and more. Essential for the study of counter-insurgency and clandestine activities. *1912, 5½ x 8½, 132 pp, soft cover. $12.00.*

☐ **19188 PERSONAL DEFENSE WEAPONS, by J. Randall.** The author, a private detective and weapons buff, evaluates all kinds of weapons: guns, knives, gas canisters, martial arts weapons, and many others — by asking some very interesting questions: Is it too deadly to use? Is it illegal to carry? Can it be comfortably concealed? How much skill does it take? Is it reliable? Whatever your situation, this practical book will help you find protection you can live with. *1992, 5½ x 8½, 102 pp, soft cover.* $12.00.

☐ **34040 SILENCING SENTRIES, by Oscar Diaz Cobo.** Oscar Diaz Cobo shows how to take out a sentry without making a sound. He should know. He's instructed members of the elite military forces and security agents in the art of close combat. Learn how to approach a sentry, what his weak points are, how to remove him, what defenses he will likely use, and more! Dozens of incredible photographs, illustrate this well-written manual. *1988, 5½ X 8½, 92 pp, illustrated, soft cover.* $14.95.

☐ **19197 STREET SMARTS FOR THE NEW MILLENNIUM, by Jack Luger.** Life can be risky for the average citizen. There are criminal elements in our society, as well as pitfalls in our everyday life, which pose real dangers to the safety and security of our families and ourselves. In this unique book, author Jack Luger has provided the methods and resources that enable the reader to minimize these threats to our lives, liberties, and pursuit of happiness. You'll learn to: depend on personal resources instead of police; protect yourself, your family, and your assets; and earn untraceable income. So don't be a victim! Learn to be self-reliant, and arm yourself with the knowledge that it takes to develop your street smarts and survive this dangerous decade! *1996, 5½ x 8½, 138 pp, soft cover.* $15.00.

☐ **19205 KILL-AS-CATCH-CAN: Wrestling Skills for Streetfighting, by Ned Beaumont.** Sure, you know how to punch and kick, but how well can you fight at shorter range? When both you and your opponent are rolling around and wrestling on the barroom floor, are you confident you can win the fight? If you doubt your chances at close quarters, then you're not prepared for the reality of streetfighting. This no-nonsense primer offers an enhanced awareness of wrestling's methodology, and provides streetfighters with the winning edge it takes to come out on top. By reading this book and employing the methods it describes, you can gain a superior edge in future altercations. *1998, 5½ x 8½, 208 pp, illustrated, soft cover.* $16.95.

☐ **32059 WIDE OPEN TO TERRORISM, by Tony Lesce.** American society (and most of the Western world) is *Wide Open to Terrorism!* The World Trade Center, Oklahoma City bombing, the derailment of an Amtrak Sunrise Unlimited train, and numerous other terrorist attacks in the recent past are irrefutable evidence of this. Topics covered include: the nature and history of terrorism; our appalling vulnerabilities; disruption techniques; computer sabotage; kidnapping; assassination; self-protection; and much, much more! *1996, 5½ x 8½, 250 pp, illustrated, indexed, soft cover.* $18.95.

☐ 88888 **LOOMPANICS UNLIMITED MAIN CATALOG**, Packed with over 230 pages of more than 700 of the most controversial and unusual titles ever printed! *8½ x 11, 234 pages, profusely illustrated, soft cover.* $5.00 (*Free* if order with any of the above titles.)

Please send me the books I have checked below:

☐ 19246, **The New Bullwhip Book**, $12.95

☐ 19103, **The Sling**, $8.95

☐ 19216, **The Scourge of the Dark Continent**, $8.95

☐ 32060, **David's Tool Kit**, $16.95

☐ 32039, **Night Movements**, $12.00

☐ 19188, **Personal Defense Weapons**, $12.00

☐ 34040, **Silencing Sentries**, $14.95

☐ 19197, **Street Smarts for The Millennium**, $15.00

☐ 19205, **Kill-As-Catch-Can**, $16.95

☐ 32059, **Wide Open to Terrorism**, $18.95

☐ 88888, **Loompanics Main Catalog**, $5.00 (*FREE* if ordered with any of the above titles. Check out our catalog ad on the next page.)

**Loompanics Unlimited
PO Box 1197
Port Townsend, WA 98368**

BC5

Please send me the books I have checked above. I have enclosed $_____ which includes $6.25 for shipping and handling of the first $25 ordered. Add an additional $1 shipping for each additional $25 ordered. Washington residents include 8.3% sales tax.

Name _____

Address_____

City/State/Zip _____

**We accept Visa, Discover, MasterCard and American Express.
1-800-380-2230 for credit card orders *only*.
24 hours a day, 7 days a week.**

Check out our Web site for more titles:

www.loompanics.com